LEEK

50 YEARS AGO: 1

Lindsey Porter

Lindsey Porter

Photography by Arthur Goldstraw

Published by
Guidelines Books & Sales
11 Belmont Road, Ipstones, Stoke on Trent ST10 2JN
Tel: 07971 990 649
Email: author.porter@gmail.com

ISBN: 978-1-84306-556-2

Print: Berforts Information Press, Eynsham, Oxford
Design: Mark Titterton

Captions

Front cover: Bowling Green Inn

Back cover: Clerk Bank

Page 1: Church Street with the Britannia Mill chimney behind

Page 3 Title page: All Saints Church of England (Aided) First School, Compton/Southbank

The photos on pp69, 70 bottom and 71 top were taken by G Walwyn (Basil Jeuda Collection). Page 28 is believed to have been a work's photo.

LEEK

50 YEARS AGO: 1

Lindsey Porter

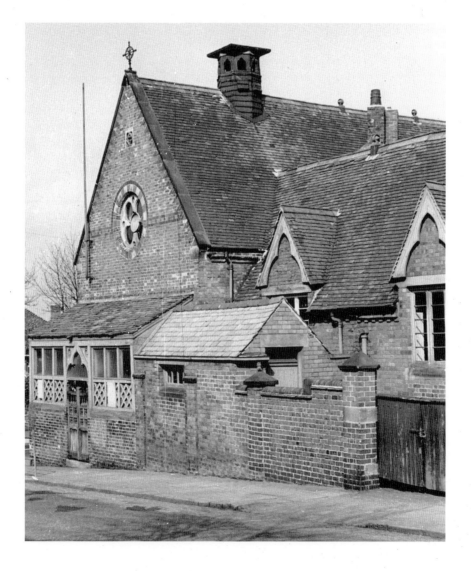

Photography by Arthur Goldstraw

An evocative photograph taken from the top of St Edward's Church tower. The tall chimney on the right is at Stephen Goodwin and Tatton's Britannia Mill, which faced West Street and St Stephen's Square (facing the camera). It was destroyed by fire in the early 1940s. Apparently, German bombers flew over the town the night before and the night after the fire, but not on the night the mill burnt down. The burnt out building existed for many years after the war, until the tax office development saw the remains swept away. Underneath the chimney was a well, thought to have been as deep as the chimney was high and it was the highest in Leek, even after it had been lowered. The mill in the centre with the conical top to the tower was Lux Lux, facing the Slimma factory seen to the left. The chimney far left, was at S. Mayer's Euston Mill in Wellington Street, which also burnt down, (see p. 65). The buildings behind the houses fronting Overton Bank have all gone, with the exception of Field House, formerly the National Club. In the 1960s, the Wallbridge estate did not exist.

The cottages adjacent to the entry from Mill Street rising to Belle Vue, with the Ragged School on the right, now apartments.

An overview of the various cottages seen above.

The Ragged School and one of the many shops in the street, all of which and Ron Deville's motor cycle shop, have all now gone.

An evocative view of the entry or passageway to Belle Vue with a gas light. The latter were sold to an American antique dealer, who bought them from Norman Ash, one of the town's jewellers.

Mill Street from near the former Co-op (see below). The advertising hoardings front Wheatley's Builder's Yard, a site of cottages demolished before the 1960s.

Properties removed to reduce the bend in the road, including the Co-op, seen here, and the Blue Ball Inn.

A former milling stone, probably from the old water mill after which the street gets its name. Did its position here mark the house of the miller? The car in the scene 15 (top) is parked over the stone.

This much older postcard shows the demolished cottages (painted white) and the millstone appears to be adjacent the second tree.

The Blue Ball Inn.

The cottages next to the inn, which is on the left.

The next group of scenes show the opposite side of the street. This used to be the smallest house in Leek. It was just 6ft 6inches wide (2m). It was derelict by the early 1960s.

The smallest house was next to Pedleys, who lived here. The site of the little house was by the white gate.

Cottages on both sides of the street just above Big Mill. The ones on the left are believed to have gone when the photo of No. 55 (see pp 10-11) were taken. This image is a little older than 1960.

The three story house on the last photo is just visible on the left. The white building further down the street is the former Nag's Head pub, see below.

Ron Deville's motor cycle shop, the former Nag's Head Inn. This building still survives today, one of the better quality buildings erected in the street. The front of the building marks the street frontage in former times.

These buildings existed just below the Nag's Head Inn. The gap just beyond the car marks Mill Street Square, some old and poor quality cottages and shops around the square. BELOW The site of these cottages can be identified by the replacement housing on the left.

All these properties have gone except the small detached one, which had another behind it, which is also still there. These were opposite the Blue Ball Inn/Co-op. The building on the far left is also on the far left of the scene below.

Looking up the street, Mill Street Square is where the lorry is parked. Ron's Motor Cycle Shop is just behind it. The property just in front of the lorry is being demolished. Notice the barber's pole. The Blue Ball Inn is on the right.

One of the few commercially built properties on the street frontage (ignoring shops and pubs). The far right door is interesting as it is wide enough for a horse.

The last three story property in the street, heading west, with its shade on the top floor.

Cottages at the Mill Street corner with Abbey Green Road.

Cottages near to Abbey Green Road, showing part of Hencroft Works. It was here that William Morris and Bernard Wardle discovered vegetable dyes and revolutionised the dyeing industry.

The Conservative Club and the cottage next to the corn mill.

The old corn mill, now the Brindley Mill.

The junction of Mill Street with Macclesfield Road and Belle Vue. The shop has now gone, plus the cottages visible higher up the street. On the left side is Hope silk mill.

MACCLESFIELD ROAD

The Dyer's Arms. The cottages on the right have now been demolished. Behind the terrace was the remains of a substantial stone built building. This has also now been cleared away.

Installing new equipment at Hope Mill in 1959. The buildings to the left have gone and the site is now part of the Sainsbury site. The graceful chimney at Sir T and A Wardle's dyeworks has also gone.

KILN LANE

This old road ran from the Dyer's Arms to Wallbridge, the original road disappearing in the Wallgrange estate. The lime kiln remains near to the junction, close to where these cottages existed.

ABBEY GREEN ROAD

The current Abbey Inn was the Bowling Green in the early 1960s. John Prince was the landlord when this scene was taken, before the current patio was built. The name came from the monk's bowling green, held to have been nearby.

ABOVE
The Hermit's Cave, Abbey Green (no public access).

LEFT
A carved head from the bottom of an arch from the former abbey church built into current buildings at Abbey Green farm, seen in 1962 (no public access).

In the 1960s, water pipes were laid down the valley from Tittesworth reservoir towards Stoke-on-Trent. It is interesting to note the equipment then in use.

Two further views of the new pipeline.

Cottages at Abbey Green Road and Broad's Bridge.

This bridge was the original access to Leek Alexandra Football Club's ground. The later was built over by Sir T & A Wardle, as the company's dyeing business grew. It still exists, just upstream from the Brindley Mill, with new bridges on either side.

The weir adjacent to the Brindley Mill (this is a new name, introduced since its conversion to a museum). The mill wheel is off to the right.

CHURCH STREET

Church Street had a narrow roadway, particularly at the Market Place end and was widened to cope with increased traffic. It originally had another 4-storey building running lengthways into the Market Place beyond the Golden Lion Inn.

Tha archway gave access to the inn's yard.

Ernie Carter's shop extended into the next property and sold clothing, bedding etc.

Next came this small stone built property in use as a fruit and flower shop.

The large stone faced building in the middle of the street was the Conservative Club, with Mrs Cumberlidge's hat shop adjoining. Below this was the former coaching inn, the George Hotel. The bottom view also includes the Swan Hotel, now (since 2013) the Green Dragon Inn.

ABOVE
The former view of the Old Church (St Edward's) showing how narrow was the roadway. This view has recently changed with the removal of most of the trees. The roots had made the wall unstable and at the time of writing (Spring 2014), the wall is being rebuilt.

LEFT
A reminder of the now stolen ducking stool which stood on the south side of the church nave. It would be nice is some benevolent carpenter could re-create what we have lost.

ST EDWARD STREET

The Swan Hotel, now called the Green Dragon, the inn's original name. It was held with land to the west. Picton Street was originally named Dragon Street and the small clump of trees beyond the last house on the right in Westwood Road (adjacent to the former Primary School site) is Dragon's Croft. In this scene, the nearest shop is selling furniture; neither shop displays its proprietor's name.

The former street frontage down to Strangman's Street before the GPO buildings were built.

The former Westminster Bank (now Bank House) and Parker's brewery tied house, The Wilkes's Head. In the 1960s, there were only five inns in the country with this name. The inn sign had a better image of John Wilkes, who was cross-eyed. Around his head were the words 'North Briton' and 'No. 45', the issue of his newspaper which so incensed the king and raised the flag for freedom of the press. As a result, Wilkes spent the 1760s in Paris and on the run.

A similar view but including Stannard's shoe shop and Norman Ash's jewellers shop. Norman bought up many of Leek's old gas lamps and sold them to an American antiques dealer. By sheer co-incidence, I found myself sitting next to this gentleman on a flight to Nashville from Chicago in 1980.

The pedimented three story butcher's shop of Sam Godwin and the building below it were removed in c. 1963 for a replacement GPO (General Post Office) to replace the one on the corner of Strangman Street (see below). On the right, the corner shop was occupied by Pickford's, grocers.

The reverse view of these shops.

The former GPO. It replaced the former Black Lion Inn when Strangman Street (pronounced Strangeman) was built in 1887-88.

Street frontages in the lower part of St Edward Street. Notice the lack of cars, although these photos were taken on a Sunday.

The George Hotel, opposite the Swan Hotel, home of the Jazz Club.

Another view of this popular inn, with the town's D-I-Y shop adjacent. Was this Mr Mountford's shop?

The three-storey former Wheatsheaf Inn, a Sugden designed property at the bottom of Stanley Street, It has since lost its top floor. It was delicensed before the 1960s and my father maintained that it had the longest bar in the town.

SHEEP MARKET

Home Aids kitchen-ware shop on the corner of the street with the reverse view towards the Westminster Bank.

CLERK BANK

The building on the left was the former Beehive pub and has since been demolished. It was quite a substantial structure situated next to the entrance to the Methodist chapel.

Clerk Bank looking towards the former West Street Working Mens' Club at the top of Mill Street and West Street.

The side of the Methodist chapel and grave yard from Clerk Bank.

The former lodge to Brow Hill House, situated opposite the properties in the above photograph. This and the main house were demolished by Leek Urban District Council after purchase in 1959.

CHURCH LANE

Church Lane from St Edward Street.

Properties opposite the Church Lane entrance into the church yard.

PETTY FRANCE

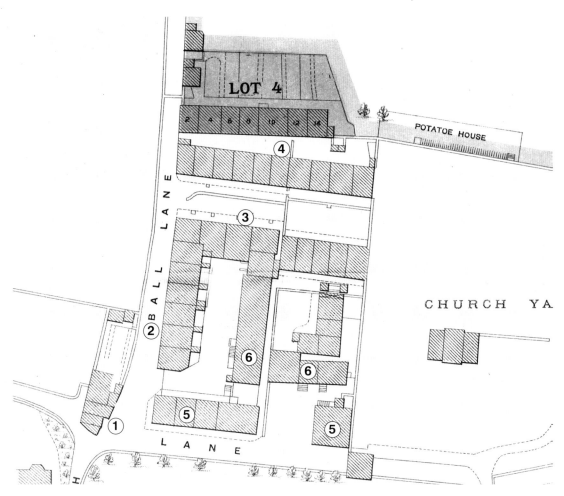

The numbers on the map mark the location of properties shown below.

(1) This house is the only remaining house at Petty France.

CONTENTS

INTRODUCTION

At least twenty years ago, I published a small book entitled Leek Thirty Years Ago. Reminded recently that we are now 50 years on from the date the photographs were taken, it seemed appropriate to consider what could be done now, reflecting how our town looked then. At that time, I accompanied my maternal godfather and uncle, Arthur Goldstraw as he photographed properties due for demolition in slum clearance schemes under the Housing Act 1956. Additional properties were lost to road widening schemes, commercial development, redundancy (the railway, canal and gas works, for example) and even fire.

His photography has left us with such an important record of physical change in terms of Leek's buildings roughly fifty years ago. It would have been very helpful if he could have looked into the future at the loss of our textile industry for instance. There were other changes too, with the last of the horse drawn traffic, the end of our love affair with steam generated in factories by coal fired stationary steam engines – hence all those chimneys which peppered the town's skyline. Much of this ended unrecorded, let alone the technical changes in the former mills.

My uncle's record has helped in the various publications I have published on Leek and the Staffordshire Moorlands. This is the first time that they have been brought together along with others never published before. They have been divided into two books. This the first, mainly covers the streets west of the Market Place. The latter and the area to the east will be in volume two.

A few images date from the 1950s and a couple are older, but used for illustrative purposes. This is the definitive collection of photographs of Leek fifty years ago.

The 1960s images were taken with a Kodak Retina 1A camera using 35mm mono film developed at home and with a Western Master light meter. He would have loved the photographic options available today together with the advances in photography brought about by improved lenses, digital cameras etc.

Lindsey Porter, Spring 2014.

MILL STREET

In the early 1960s, much of the old housing facing the street still existed, although some had already gone, eg below the Ragged School and those at the top of the north side of the street. The lady on the right is outside what was then the smallest house in Leek. The white building on the left near the cyclist was the West Street Working Mens' Club, which had a large billiard room on the first floor. In front of it stands the former toilets. The large building in the distance is Big Mill, built in 1857.

The site of the demolished Royal Oak Inn, with the rear cottages of West Street Square above, blocking the view of West Street School. The large mill is Wardle and Davenport's which was to close in the early 1970s.

A similar view showing the properties either side of the entrance to Donkey Bank Steps, situated where the barrier is erected on the pavement.

Here the Donkey Bank Steps may be seen climbing up to School Street and Belle Vue. Note the gas lamp not yet replaced. The hoarding on the left is advertising Oulton Park racetrack near Chester. Note the covers on the chimneys also.

Another view of the same group of cottages. One of the houses is already boarded up and properties opposite have already gone.

Below the cottages seen on the last page was the last row above Big Mill, including 55 Mill Street on the left, which became the smallest house following demolition of the one mentioned above, which was six inches narrower.

A close up of No. 55.

The terrace adjacent to No.55, with the whole scene dominated by the mill behind.

Big Mill and the Kings Arms Inn. The latter building later became The Jester before becoming delicensed.

The King's Arms and the view to the Ragged School.

The complex of buildings at Wardle and Davenport's mill completely dominated Mill Street.

VIEWS OVER THE TOWN

These views were taken from the top of the Nicholson Institute in 1958.

From St Luke's Church: the mill to the right is Brough Nicholson & Hall. The large mill and chimney to the left is Alexandra Mill in Queen Street. The long building further left is Worthington's mill in Portland Street/Queen Street.

PAGE 91

In the foreground the terrace is Cruso Yard, looking out onto Cavendish Square. The elegant building (left of middle) is Foxlowe, with its bowling green far right. Beyond Foxlowe is The Vicarage. The white gabled building was east of The Golden Lion and projected towards the Market Place.

PAGE 92

The Monument with the Fountain Street chapel in the foreground. Behind the latter is the Cattle Market with the Coffee Tavern behind the chapel spire. Derby Street is to the right.

This intriguing photograph shows Leek from the Park. Note the houses of Petty France below the Church tower. What, however is the tall building just left of mid-photo? And where is the Nicholson Institute? Hidden by the trees perhaps. With the Clemasha Brothers and Birch mill chimney pinpointing the mill off to the right, was this tall building in Union Street? Then there is another query: what is the flat area on the left? It appears to be too far to the left to be the lawn at the rear of Foxlowe or the New Stockwell House building, then the home of the Leek and Moorland's Building Society.

A final view of the Park and Ball Haye Hall (from the rear side).

Ball Haye Hall from the Park bowling green.

The Challinor Fountain dates from 1876 and stood originally in the Market Place before being moved to the Park. It has now been moved again to the forecourt of Moorland House, off Stockwell Street.

THE BROUGH PARK

Ball Haye Hall, now the site of the leisure centre. The carpark is on the field. The Park is basically the former gardens of the Hall.

A pleasant scene looking towards Park Vale from the gated Park Road entrance.

(2) The view down Ball Lane.

(4) Court No. 1.

(3) The first (i.e. the one nearest to the church) of the two lower terraces.

(6) Further houses beyond those visible below.

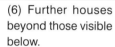

(5) Properties facing the church in Church Lane, at the top of Ball Lane.

OVERTON BANK

Note the properties in Church Street top left, which have now gone. The advert hoardings advise that performing at the Theatre Royal, Hanley was Sonia Dresdel in 'S for Scandal', which presumably was based on Richard Sheridan's late 18th century play 'School for Scandal', loosely based on the 5th Duke of Devonshire and his wife Georgiana.

The adverts promote the November Horse fair on the Haywood Street Cattle Market. Opening a bazaar for the Labour Party at the Town Hall in Market Street was Mrs Bessie Braddock, MP for Liverpool Exchange. There were films on at the Grand, Majestic and Regal cinemas. The Palace was renamed the Regal in c. 1960. The latter and the Grand were in High Street, the Majestic in Union Street. The image is damaged.

ST STEPHEN'S SQUARE

All that remained of Stephen Goodwin and Tatton's Britannia Mill, which was gutted during the war and was a feature of West Street for many years thereafter. The nearest building housed Mr Heppinstall's cobbler's shop during the 1950s.

WEST STREET

Above the Primary School in West Street was The Square, with terraced houses on three sides of a cobbled courtyard seen above. The gable end on the right can be seen on page 8. RIGHT The left hand end of the above terrace.

The houses of the Square seen from West Street.

West Street Primary School and the site of the Square following demolition of the houses. On the left are other houses following which have also been demolished.

The entrance to School Street and houses in West Street, now the site of a carpark.

School Street, with the end wall of the school to the right and Wardle and Davenport's mill in the distance. Note the cobble stones.

BELLE VUE

A fine view of Wardle and Davenport's mill. At the far end of the street is the Britannia Inn, presumably named after Britannia Mill (see above).

The mill extended down the hill with this view taken from Garden Street.

The mill gates and older buildings at the rear. Just visible behind the trees is the roof of the lodge. Henry Goldstraw was the lodge keeper until his retirement in 1956, aged 78 years. He was the father of Arthur Goldstraw and my mother, Hope, and lived in retirement until his 88th year.

The lower part of Belle Vue, descending to the area of Low Hamle (the e is silent, probably derived from Low Hamlet) and Macclesfield Road.

The reverse view with part of Wardle's mill behind. The three storey mill in the middle of the scene survives, now converted into apartments.

The view from further down the street. The lane has all the appearance of being the access before the higher street was constructed.

Was this stone built cottage built before the brick built houses?

A close-up of the now demolished houses.

The view after demolition, with the Hencroft Works in the mid-distance. The works chimney looks similar to that at Wardle and Davenport's mill and makes one wonder if it was to the same design.

WELLINGTON STREET

S. Mayer's Euston Mill was part of the street scene in this street until its destruction in 1979. The white building is the Wellington Inn.

STATION STREET

Mr Cumberlidge with the last horse-drawn coal wagon in the town. Note the two gasometers at the gas works (see p.67).

BROAD STREET

The lovely Victoria Buildings, one of the most elegant of any group of properties in the town. The shop on the corner was A.T. Jackson's opticians. Note Axon's home furnishers shop clock in the form of a house.

This little cottage stood empty for years and was knocked down when Mellor's garage was built.

NEWCASTLE ROAD

The former gas works, taken from what is now Morrison's petrol/diesel station. The building (front left) was the coke packing shop in the early 1960s. Note the latin inscription in the brickwork: Ex Fumo Dare Lucem (out of fire comes light). At the foot of the nearest buildings was the railway line to Macclesfield.

The gasworks from Newcastle Road. The house on the left was originally the works' manager's house. Note the gasometers on the right.

LEFT
Wallbridge Farm was situated just before the bend at the foot of Ladderedge and was removed in highway improvements. Notice the ugly telephone poles which defaced many a road and street. The farm was demolished in 1974.

ABOVE AND BELOW
The reverse view, with the telegraph poles again! The advert is for Cleveland Petrol.

THE RAILWAY

A standard Class 4 No. 75030 leaving on 9th September 1966. The mill on the skyline was Thomas Whittles's mill in Strangman Street.

The same train about to pass the new cattle market. Note the Birchall playing fields in the days before the Britannia Building Society properties were built.

A Stanier loco possibly drawn up for water. The mill in the background is William Milners of Langford Street.

A 2-6-0, no. 42828 passing the gasworks. The buildings above feature on p. 66.

Stanier Class 5, 4-6-0, no. 45096 with both passengers and freight leaving Leek for Cheddleton and passing under Two Arches bridge. The latter still exists, surrounded by industrial premises.

The front of the station looking rather forlorn and awaiting demolition. This is now Morrison's main car park The station closed in 1964.

Leek Signal box and Two Arches bridge. This group of photographs were taken just prior to demolition.

The Water Tower from the down (Uttoxeter) platform.

The derelict down platform with weed growing everywhere.

The Newcastle Road bridge. You go under this railway bridge from Morrison's to reach their petrol/diesel station.

Just west of the railway station was the former canal wharf, which had been filled in by c. 1960. The site was occupied by Babe's scrap yard. In the mid-distance is the railway Water Tower.

The former Leek Arm of the Caldon Canal remained navigable however. Here is an early pleasure boat on the arm. This area is now under the industrial estate.

ALBION STREET

In the early 1960s, the textile industry in Leek was enjoying success, but that was to change before another decade had passed. Here is one of the later casualties, Messrs Anthony Ward and Co Ltd.

KING STREET

Terraced houses in King Street. Some had workers' shades above, as may be seen on the left hand side.

COMPTON

More premises with a shade above on Compton. The alms houses on the corner remain.

Opposite the scene above and on a higher level was a small group of properties known collectively as Cornhill. Those fronting Compton were in Prospect Place, which ran into Cornhill Street, as seen here. The adjacent mill was Job White's textile mill.

The reverse view of Prospect Place.

Joliffe Street, looking towards the top of the Cornhill Steps, which go down to Brook Street. The houses have now gone.

The corner of Compton with Duke Street. These properties have also now gone.

Prospect Place following the disasterous fire at Job White's mill in 1964. Following demolition work, which also included some cottages, the factory was rebuilt at a cost of £300,000 and reopened in 1965.

The Compton continuation of the properties on the corner with Duke Street. They have all been demolished.

The view from Duke Street, with clearance work well advanced.

Cornhill Street showing the area of demotion work at the mill. All the houses on both sides of the street were demolished with the exception of the last few on the top left hand side.

SOUTHBANK

All Saints C.E. (Aided) First School, known as Compton School. In 1964-65, the School was moved to new premises nearer to Birchall. The old school was demolished c. 2000.

The former Southbank Hotel, a depressing sight of what had been the town's main hotel. It became the Mulberry in 1964 and was demolished in 1971.

CONDLYFFE ROAD

The Condlyffe Alms houses. Notice the former gas lamp.

THE CEMETERY

Leek's Market Cross was 'retired' to the Cemetery from the Market Place but has now been returned to where it should be.

LEEKBROOK

A wintery day looking from Birchall towards the railway bridge over the road at Leekbrook (it is just out of sight).

ABOVE
Market Street with the Town hall (right) and opposite it, the Brunswick Chapel. Left foreground is Ford House.

PAGE 93
From the Monument: to the right are The Talbot Inn, The Cattle Market Inn and the Coffee Tavern (with white windows). The chimney in front of the latter is the Swimming Pool chimney. Left of the large chimney are the Brough's mill buildings. In the foreground is Ford Street.

The view from the church tower towards High Street, showing the former Premier garage and The Grand Cinema, with the Co-op department store to the right. You can just make out the barrel roof of the Palace cinema, which faced the Co-op, sticking out beyond Field House. Many of the properties in the Bottom right hand side have now gone.

The view towards Sheep Market, with the Catholic Church in the background and Job White's mill to the left of it.

LEEK

50 YEARS AGO: 2

LEEK
50 YEARS AGO:2

Lindsey Porter
Photographs by Arthur Goldstraw

Volume 2 will include:

Market Place
Derby Street
Russell Street
Moreton's Yard
Pickwood Road
Cattle Market
Smithfield Centre
Stockwell Street
Cruso's Yard
Union Street
Brick Bank
Buxton Road
Portland Street
Ashbourne Road
Cross Street
Smithfield Terrace
Coffee Tavern
Lowe Hill Bridge
Club Day
May Fair

Specification:

as this book; ISBN: 978 184306 5579

(Detail subject to alteration without notice)